WELCOME TO
BADLANDS
NATIONAL PARK

BY TERI AND BOB TEMPLE

Content Consultant: Marianne Mills, Chief of Resource Education, Badlands National Park

MAP KEY

The maps throughout this
book use the following icons:

🏕 Campground

🚗 Driving Excursion

🥾 Hiking Trail

❓ Information Center

🔭 Overlook

🛎 Picnic Area

✴ Point of Interest

🐾 Prairie Dog Town

👤 Ranger Station

🏠 Visitor Center

About National Parks

A national park is an area of land that has been set aside by Congress. National parks protect nature and history. In most cases, no hunting, grazing, or farming is allowed. The first national park in the United States—and in the world—was Yellowstone National Park. It is located in parts of Wyoming, Idaho, and Montana. It was founded in 1872. In 1916, the U.S. National Park Service began.

Today, the National Park Service manages more than 380 sites. Some of these sites are historic, such as the Statue of Liberty or Martin Luther King, Jr. National Historic Site. Other park areas preserve wild land. The National Park Service manages 40% of the nation's wilderness areas, including national parks. Each year, millions of people from around the world visit these national parks. Visitors may camp, go canoeing, or go for a hike. Or, they may simply sit and enjoy the scenery, wildlife, and the quiet of the land.

TABLE OF

The Child's World®

**Published in the
United States of America
by The Child's World®**

PO Box 326
Chanhassen, MN 55317-0326
800-599-READ
www.childsworld.com

Acknowledgements
The Child's World®: Mary Berendes,
Publishing Director

The Design Lab: Kathleen Petelinsek,
Design and Page Production

Map Hero, Inc.: Matt Kania, Cartographer

Red Line Editorial: Bob Temple, Editorial
Direction

Photo Credits
Cover and this page: Pat O'Hara/Corbis.

Interior: BrandXPictures: 10 (bottom), 14–
15, 25; Corbis: 17, 25; David Muench/
Corbis: 1, 2–3; Dick Kettlewell/Getty: 11;
Edward S. Curtis/Corbis: 10 (top), 19;
Layne Kennedy/Corbis: 7, 8, 9, 22–23,

**Library of Congress
Cataloging-in-Publication Data**
Temple, Teri.
 Welcome to Badlands National Park /
by Teri Temple and Bob Temple.
  p. cm. — (Visitor guides)
 Includes index.
 ISBN 1-59296-693-4 (library bound : alk.
paper)
 1. Badlands National Park (S.D.)—Juvenile
literature. I. Temple, Bob. II. Title. III. Series.
 F657.B24T46 2006
 917.83'93—dc22   2005030079

On the cover and this page
A sunny day shows off the layers of
differently colored rocks in Badlands
National Park.

On page 1
The Badlands' rocky formations are
beautiful at sunrise.

On pages 2–3
Prairie grass grows in many places of
Badlands National Park.

WELCOME TO BADLANDS NATIONAL PARK

Λ

🚶

Strange and Beautiful

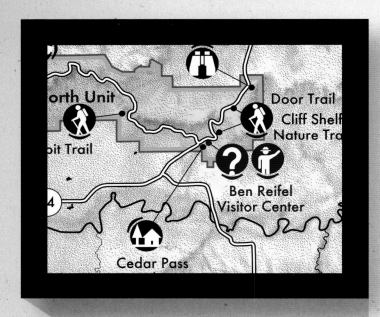

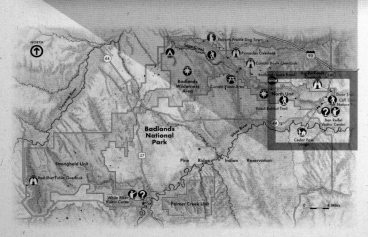

Welcome to Badlands National Park! This is a beautiful part of south-western South Dakota. Here you will find strange rock formations and endless prairies.

Created over millions of years, this rocky landscape is always changing. In a process called erosion, wind and rain wear away the soil. Erosion creates the deep canyons and odd peaks that make up the Badlands. It allows us to see the colorful layers in the rock. These layers represent different time periods from the past.

A good place to start your visit is at the Ben Reifel Visitor Center. It is located near an entrance to the park. Here you'll find everything you need for your adventures. Join a ranger on a hike to learn about the land. Grab a map and backpack cross-country like the pioneers. Be sure to bring a pair of binoculars!

SOUTH DAKOTA

Badlands National Park

These rounded hills were formed by thousands of years of erosion. They continue to erode today; rain hits the tops of the hills and rolls down the cracks and the "wrinkles." Each raindrop carries away a little bit more of the hills.

A lone bison grazes in the Badlands Wilderness Area. This area is the largest wild prairie in the United States. More than 500 bison make their home here. Adult bison can grow to be more than 6 feet (1.8 m) high at the shoulder and weigh 2,000 pounds (907 kg).

A Bigger Place

Badlands National Park is divided into three areas called units. The North Unit is the most popular. It is home to Badlands Wilderness Area and hundreds of giant bison. You can also drive along the Badlands Loop Road. It has many scenic **overlooks** and easy hiking trails.

The Stronghold and Palmer Creek units are located on the Pine Ridge Indian **Reservation**, home to the people of the Oglala Lakota Nation. Badlands National Park works with the Lakota to take care of these special areas. You can learn more about Native American history in the Badlands at the White River Visitor Center. The only sound you hear is the wind—and maybe a coyote. At night, the stars are clear and bright.

The park's three units make a kind of crescent shape. See page 28 for a larger picture of the three units.

9

Oglala Lakota

Native Americans have been a part of the Great Plains for thousands of years. When white settlers first arrived in the mid-1800s, South Dakota's Badlands region was the home of the Oglala Lakota people, also known as the Oglala Sioux. As time went on, the push for settlement and a gold rush in the nearby Black Hills led the U.S. government to break earlier treaties and force the Lakota from most of their lands. Today, nearly 18,000 Oglala Lakota tribal members live on the Pine Ridge Reservation, which includes about half of Badlands National Park.

The best time to visit the park is in the early morning or evening. The colorful layers of the Badlands look their best in the soft light. That's also when the wildlife is most active. Don't miss the eagles and hawks as they soar across the cloudless sky.

🚶🚶 A **mineral** called *hematite* (which is actually rust) creates the red stripes in these hills, called the Brule (BROOL) Formation. The Brule Formation was once a series of river and stream beds.

Geological Forces

At the Big Badlands Overlook, the first thing you notice is the rocky terrain. Look over a ridge. It looks like another world, full of odd shapes and colorful rock.

How were these Badlands formed? Millions of years ago, this area was actually a shallow sea. **Geological forces** caused the sea to drain away. Subtropical forests grew. Later it became grassland, much like you see today.

Rivers and streams **deposited** layer upon layer of over the area. The deposits created mudstones, sandstones, and siltstones—some of the softest rocks on Earth. To the west, volcanoes erupted and the winds carried the ash into pockets and layers.

Livings things that died became trapped in the soil. Their **remains** became fossils. These fossils were revealed in the layers of rock as it eroded. The Badlands contain an enormous collection of fossils. Scientists travel from all over the world to study the fossils and learn about the Earth's past.

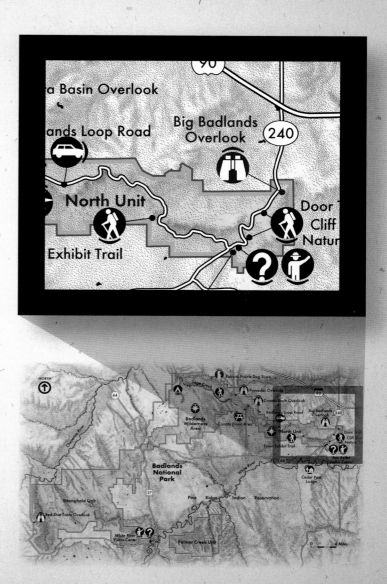

Grasslands

Don't be fooled by this **barren** landscape. The Badlands Wilderness Area supports more than just grass! Hundreds of plants and wildflowers provide a home and food to the creatures that live here.

The Badlands contain the largest protected prairie in the National Park System. Grasslands, or prairies, occur when an area is too dry for trees and too wet to be called a desert. Look for the tall green needlegrass that grows near wet areas. Shorter buffalograss prefers rockier soil.

Prairies once covered much of North America. Today, most prairies have been changed into farmland or cities. In fact, only 2 out of every 100 prairie areas remain! The Badlands' prairie is protected, which means the plants and animals living there will always be able to live in their natural state.

Adult bighorns can grow to be over 250 pounds (113 kg) and stand 40 inches (1 m) tall at the shoulder. Males fight each other by crashing their heads together—a battle that makes a cracking sound so loud that it can be heard more than a mile (1.6 km) away.

Many animals, like the bison, need lots of space to roam and grass to graze on. That makes these grasslands the perfect home for their herds. Shy bighorn sheep may graze in the open prairies, but they hide in the park's **buttes** and canyons for safety. While hiking on the trails, watch for passing pronghorn. They can be seen running through the tall prairie grasses. Today, Badlands National Park protects the largest area of native North American prairie in the National Park System.

Black-Footed Ferret

The playful black-footed ferret is the rarest **mammal** on Earth. Part of the weasel family, it was once thought to be **extinct**. Scientists were amazed to find it in the wild in Wyoming. Through a process called **reintroduction**, scientists brought black-footed ferrets back to the Badlands. Now, you can once again see them chasing their favorite food, the prairie dog!

Reclaimed Wilderness

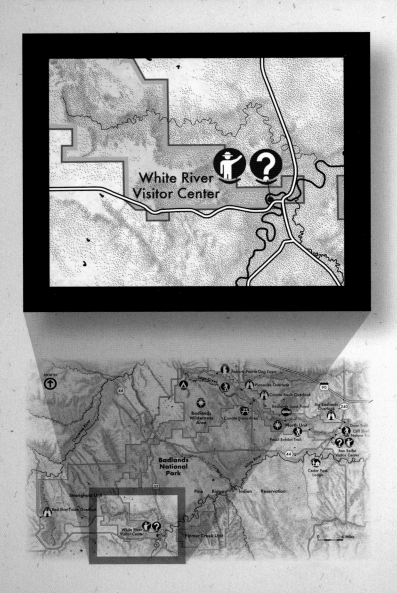

People have lived and hunted in the Badlands for more than 11,000 years. Over the centuries, different American Indian groups used the Badlands as a hunting place, but never a home. The harsh climate and lack of protection didn't make it a good year-round home. Settlers came and tried to change the land. The Badlands were not meant to be farms, however. Many of the settlers abandoned their claims because of the hard land and climate.

Stop at either visitor center in the park. Learn more about these pioneers called homesteaders, and about the American Indians. The exhibits you'll find tell of the land's exciting past. Make sure to explore the new exhibits year round, or attend a ranger program during summer. There is so much to see and do!

This famous photo, called *An Oasis in the Badlands*, was taken by Edward Curtis in 1905. It shows sub-chief Red Hawk, an Oglala Lakota (Sioux) leader and warrior. Red Hawk took part in 20 battles, including the famous 1876 Battle of the Little Bighorn.

Over 400 different kinds of plants can be found in the park. The sunflower, a native wildflower, grows in many areas. In large numbers, these flowers create a welcoming sight. The sunflower is named for its ability to turn its "face" to follow the sun throughout the day.

Settler's Accidental Gardens

The Homestead Act of 1862 promised free land in the western areas of the United States. As people from around the world moved across the area, they brought with them memories of home—plants. Settlers moving west "accidentally" brought with them seeds from plants where they came from.

Some seeds were left behind in the waste from their animals. Other seeds arrived in the cuffs of the pioneers' pants! These new plants threatened the native grasslands. Today the park is working to return the prairies to their original glory.

By 1909, the people of South Dakota began petitioning Congress. They wanted this beautiful land to be **preserved** for the future. They felt this area was more than just an endless prairie full of strange rocks. It was important to science. In 1939, the area was set aside as Badlands National Monument. In 1978, Congress renamed it Badlands National Park.

Extreme Weather

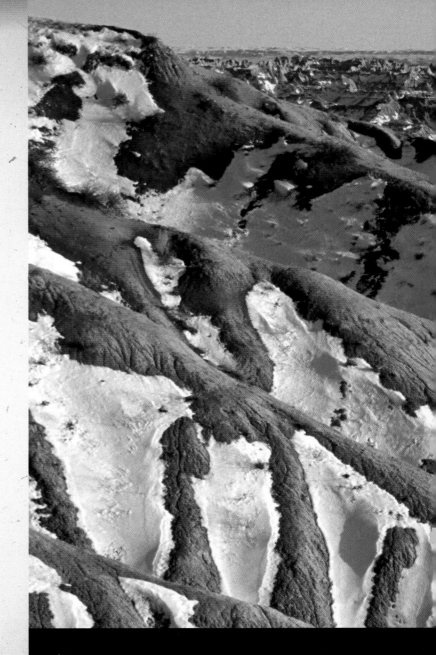

The Badlands are a land of extremes. Come prepared for surprises. Most visitors come to the park during the summer months. However, the park is open all year. There's always something exciting to do.

In summer, you will find beautiful wildflowers and lots of wildlife. Hike the trails and search for fossils. Plan a horseback ride to view the land. End your day at an evening program led by the park rangers. Make sure you're ready for hot weather and wild lightning storms.

The winter is quiet. The buttes are lightly covered with snow. Take a trip off the beaten path and visit the critters in Badlands Wilderness Area. The curious prairie dogs are sure to entertain you. You'll need to bundle up, though. The wind and cold from the north can be chilly. No matter when you visit, you will be fascinated by all that Badlands National Park has to offer.

When snow falls on the eroding hills of the Badlands, wonderful designs form. When the snow melts in spring, the water carries away more of the hills, and the erosion continues.

Roberts Prairie Dog Town

Down a dusty dirt road you will find a unique town. The town's best known **inhabitants** are furry little brown animals known as prairie dogs. They have high-pitched barks like little dogs, but they are actually cousins of the squirrel.

Prairie dogs live underground in burrows. They spend most of their days barking warnings at their neighbors. Prairie dogs are in danger, though. They need our help protecting their habitat.

Badlands Loop Road

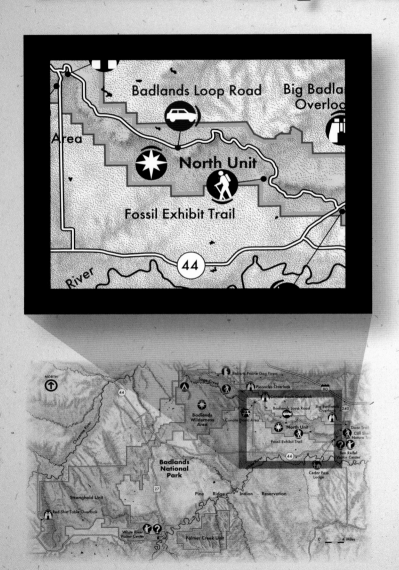

There is another way to see all the park has to offer. Take a drive along Badlands Loop Road. It runs through the North Unit, and it is open all year. There is something for every explorer along this scenic road.

Let's take a closer look at some of the best spots. An easy trail to start your journey on is the Cliff Shelf Nature Trail. It winds through one of the few wooded areas of the prairie. Be sure to get a pamphlet for this trail at the trailhead. It will introduce you to the plants and animals living in the Badlands.

There's also Door Trail. Walk through a natural doorway into the Badlands on this route. Instead of a formal trail, it is marked by small yellow markers. For the more daring adventurers, there is Notch Trail. Hike into a canyon, climb up a ladder, and walk along a narrow canyon rim. It's a tough climb, but you will be rewarded with one of the best views in the park!

As you travel west, plan a hike down Fossil Exhibit Trail. Among the fragile rocks you will see replicas of the fossils that were found in this area!

...n years old. It was found in the White River Badlands of South Dakota—an area known for its huge number of mammal ...mmals have been discovered here, ranging from tiny rodents to the huge *Titanothere*—an animal the size of an elephant.

End your day with a picnic at Conata Basin Overlook. Be sure to check out the **paleontologists** at the Big Pig Dig from mid-June to mid-August. You can watch them work at the site as they uncover fossils. If you find a fossil in the park, be sure to tell a park ranger. It might help unravel a mystery from the past!

Badlands National Park may seem empty. However, it is full of life and traces of the past. Rocky terrain surrounds you. A butterfly rests on a wildflower. A coyote stalks its prey. Bison roam the grasslands. These are the simple pleasures of the Badlands.

The Big Pig Dig

Each summer in the Badlands, you can see paleontologists at work. Paleontologists study fossils to learn about the past. In 1993, bones were found near a picnic area in the park. Scientists thought they belonged to an ancient pig. They discovered instead that they belonged to an ancient rhinoceros! These small rhinos once lived in the Badlands. The Pig Dig is next to the Conata Picnic Area.

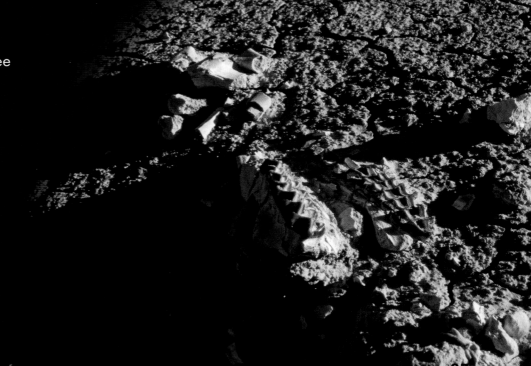

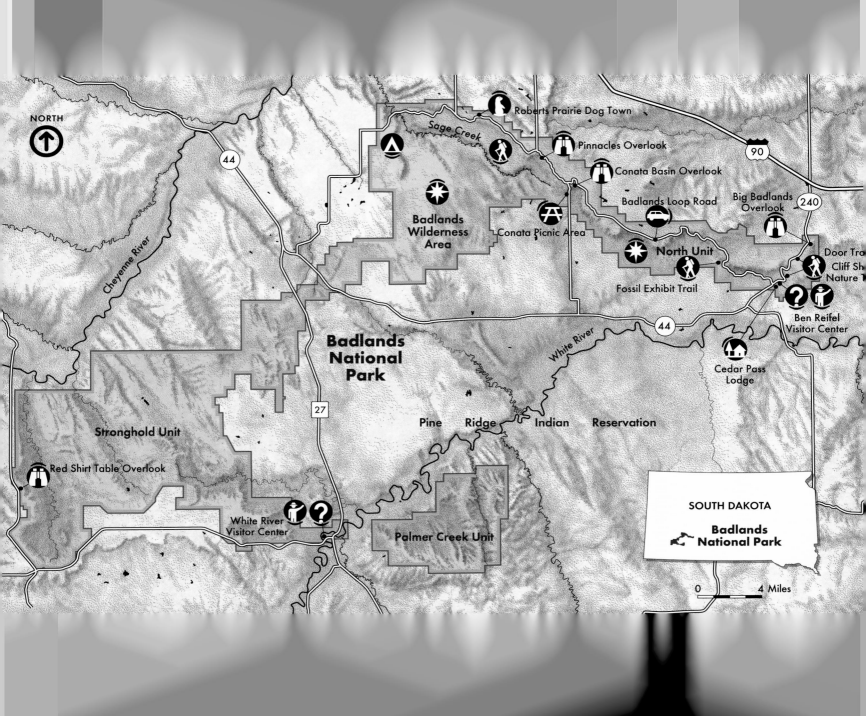

NORTH

44

Cheyenne River

Sage Creek

Roberts Prairie Dog Town

Pinnacles Overlook

Conata Basin Overlook

Badlands Loop Road

Big Badlands Overlook

90

240

Badlands Wilderness Area

Conata Picnic Area

North Unit

Fossil Exhibit Trail

Door Tra
Cliff Sh
Nature T

Ben Reifel
Visitor Center

44

Badlands National Park

White River

Cedar Pass Lodge

Stronghold Unit

27

Pine   Ridge   Indian   Reservation

Red Shirt Table Overlook

White River
Visitor Center

Palmer Creek Unit

SOUTH DAKOTA

Badlands
National Park

0   4 Miles

BADLANDS NATIONAL PARK FAST FACTS

Date founded: January 25, 1939

Location: Southwestern South Dakota

Size: 379 square miles/982 sq km; 242,560 acres/98,161 hectares

Major habitats: Grasslands and rocky terrain

Important landforms: Rock formations: canyons, buttes, spires, pinnacles, gorges, gullies, and peaks

Elevation:
   Highest: 3,247 feet/990 m (Pinnacles Overlook)
   Lowest: 2,443 feet/745 m (Visitor's Center)

Weather:
   Average yearly rainfall: 15.6 inches/39.6 cm
   Average temperatures: 67 F/19.4 C to 37 F/2.8 C

Number of animal species: 60 species of mammals, 215 types of birds, and 20 species of amphibians and reptiles

Main animal species: Black-tailed prairie dogs, mule deer, pronghorn (antelope), bison, bighorn sheep, coyotes, hawks, eagles, and turtles

Number of plant species: 470 types of plants, 60 types of mixed grasses, and hundreds of wildflowers

Main plant species: Grasses: buffalograss or big bluestem

Number of endangered or threatened animal/plant species: 1—black-footed ferret

Native people: Oglala Lakota

Number of visitors each year: More than 1.2 million

Important sites and landmarks: Badlands Loop Road trails and overlooks, Ben Reifel Visitor Center, Cedar Pass Lodge, Badlands Wilderness Area, and Roberts Prairie Dog Town

Tourist activities: Ranger-led programs, hiking, camping, backpacking, picnicking, and horseback riding

GLOSSARY

barren (BAYR-ren): Land that can grow few, if any, plants and trees on it is barren. Much of the Badlands is rocky and barren.

buttes (BYOOTS): Buttes are steep mountains or hills with flat tops. In Badlands National Park, you can climb buttes and hike canyons.

deposited (deh-POS-it-ed): When something is deposited, it is placed or laid down somewhere. Volcanoes deposited layers of ash in the Badlands.

extinct (ek–STINKT): When there are no more of a particular plant or animal, it is extinct. Scientists thought the black-footed ferret was extinct, but a few were found still living.

geological forces (jee-uh-LOJ-ik-ull FOR-sez): Geological forces are earth-related activities that change the land, like a volcano erupting. Geological forces helped to form the layers in the Badlands rocks.

inhabitants (in-HAB-it-unts): The inhabitants of a place are the creatures that live there. Prairie dogs are inhabitants of the Badland prairie.

mammal (MAM-ull): A mammal is an animal that has hair on its body and feeds its babies milk from its body. Black-footed ferrets, people, cows, and dogs are all mammals.

mineral (MIN-er-ull): A mineral is a natural material that is not a plant nor an animal. Hematite is a mineral.

overlooks (OV-er-looks): Overlooks are places that allow you to look down on something. You will get a beautiful view of the Badlands at Pinnacles Overlook.

paleontologists (pay-lee-un-TOL-uh-jists): Paleontologists are scientists who study signs of ancient life such as fossils. Paleontologists work on finding more bones at the Big Pig Dig in the Badlands.

preserved (preh-ZURVD): When you preserve something you are protecting it so it stays unchanged and unharmed. The U.S. people wanted to preserve the Badlands.

reintroduction (ree-in-truh-DUK-shun): Reintroduction is increasing an animal's numbers in an area where it has died out or become scarce. To do that, the animals are raised in zoos or parks and then released into the wild. Black-footed ferrets were brought back to the Badlands using reintroduction.

remains (reh-MAYNZ): The parts of something that were once alive are its remains. Fossils are the remains of the animals that once lived in the Badlands.

reservation (reh-zur-VAY-shun): A reservation is an area of land set aside by the government for a special purpose. The Pine Ridge Indian Reservation is located next to Badlands National Park.

TO FIND OUT MORE

Λ

FURTHER READING

Cerney, Jan and Janice Brozik Cerney.
Badlands National Park (Images of America).
Mount Pleasant, SC: Arcadia Publishing, 2004.

Nelson, S.D.
The Star People: A Lakota Story.
New York: Harry N. Abrams, 2003.

Silverstein, Alvin and Virginia Silverstein.
The Black-Footed Ferret.
Brookfield, CT: Millbrook Press, 1995.

Wade, Linda L.
Badlands: Beauty Carved from Nature.
Vero Beach, FL: Rourke, 1991.

ON THE WEB

Visit our home page for lots of links about
Badlands National Park:

http://www.childsworld.com/links

NOTE TO PARENTS, TEACHERS, AND LIBRARIANS:
We routinely check our Web links to make sure
they're safe, active sites—so encourage your
readers to check them out!

INDEX